Inspiration and Guidance for Daily Living

A *Jesus in My Pocket* Book

And whenever you stand praying,
if you have anything against anyone,
forgive him, that your Father in heaven
may also forgive you your trespasses.

Mark 11:25

Thomas Nelson Publishers
Nashville

The Forgiving Heart
Inspiration and Guidance for Daily Living
A *Jesus in My Pocket* Book

Jesus in My Pocket Ministries
PMB #327
6632 Telegraph Road
Bloomfield, MI 48301

Printed in Mexico
1 2 3 4 5 6 . . . 04 03 02 01 00 99

When I forgive from my heart...

My relationships improve. As I practice lovingkindness and forgiveness, I know I am carrying out the will of God.

God's Word says...

If there is any other commandment, are all summed up in this saying, namely, "You shall love your neighbor as yourself." Love does no harm to a neighbor; therefore love is the fulfillment of the law.

Romans 13:9-10

Jesus in My Pocket

Just for You

Fold Here

FROM: ____________________

TO: ____________________

____

When I forgive from my heart...

I forgive those who humiliate me. I search my soul to see if I have willingly caused them pain, and I turn to God for consolation. I know, as His child, I need never feel ashamed.

God's Word says...

The LORD your God in your midst,
The Mighty One, will save;
He will rejoice over you with gladness,
He will quiet you with His love,
He will rejoice over you with singing.

Zephaniah 3:17

Jesus in My Pocket

Just for You

Fold Here

FROM: ____________

TO: ____________

____

When I forgive from my heart...

I hold no grudges. Knowing that only love should fill me, I forgive freely and easily. I let go of all negative emotions towards others as soon as I feel them surfacing within me.

God's Word says...

Bless those who persecute you; bless and do not curse.

Romans 12:14

Jesus in My Pocket

Just for You

Fold Here

FROM: ____________________

TO: ____________________

____

When I forgive from my heart...

I forgive those who do not comfort me when I am sad. I will try to put on a happy face, put my trust in God's salvation, and remember that sometimes people are unable to comfort me because they are too sad themselves.

God's Word says...

Though the fig tree may not blossom,
Nor fruit be on the vines;
Though the labor of the olive may fail,
And the fields yield no food; . . .
Yet I will rejoice in the LORD,
I will joy in the God of my salvation.

Habakkuk 3:17-18

Jesus in My Pocket

Just for You

Fold Here

FROM: ____________

TO: ____________

____

When I forgive from my heart...

I forgive those in authority over me for any harm they may have caused me, whether emotional or physical. As I grow in love with Jesus, my forgiving heart knows no boundaries.

God's Word says...

As the elect of God, holy and beloved, put on tender mercies, kindness, humility, meekness, longsuffering; bearing with one another, and forgiving one another, if anyone has a complaint against another; even as Christ forgave you, so you also must do. But above all these things put on love, which is the bond of perfection.

Colossians 3:12-14

Just for You

Jesus in My Pocket

Fold Here

FROM: ____________

TO: ____________

____

When I forgive from my heart...

I forgive those under my authority who won't heed my advice. I offer words of wisdom from the Bible when I can, and allow God to do the rest.

God's Word says...

Righteous lips are the delight of kings,
And they love him who speaks what is
right.

Proverbs 16:13

Just for You

Jesus in My Pocket

Fold Here

FROM: ____________________

TO: ____________________

____

When I forgive from my heart...

I release all anxiety. I do not cling to thoughts that are not pure and loving. I remember that Jesus is with me every step of the way, but He asks that I leave my worries behind.

God's Word says...

Be anxious for nothing, but in everything by prayer and supplication, with thanksgiving, let your requests be made known to God; and the peace of God, which surpasses all understanding, will guard your hearts and minds through Christ Jesus.

Philippians 4:6-7

Jesus in My Pocket

Just for You

Fold Here

FROM: ____________________

TO: ____________________

____

When I forgive from my heart...

I forgive those who take advantage of me. I know I cannot change another person's behavior, but I can forgive them, look at my own behavior, and make sure I do not take advantage of others.

God's Word says...

Therefore I take pleasure in infirmities, in reproaches, in needs, in persecutions, in distresses, for Christ's sake. For when I am weak, then I am strong.

2 Corinthians 12:10

Jesus in My Pocket

Just for You

Fold Here

FROM: ____________________

TO: ____________________

____

When I forgive from my heart...

I forgive those who treat me unfairly. My family, my boss, my coworkers, my neighbors—whoever may be less than fair to me—deserves my forgiveness, even if I feel like being unfair to them in return.

God's Word says...

For we know Him who said, "Vengeance is Mine, I will repay," says the Lord. And again, "The LORD will judge His people."

Hebrews 10:30

Just for You

Jesus in My Pocket

Fold Here

FROM: ____________________

TO: ____________________

____

When I forgive from my heart...

I free myself to love again. Since I know my heart cannot hold on to strife and love at the same time, I release all thoughts of revenge and allow the love of God to flow through me.

God's Word says...

Hatred stirs up strife,
But love covers all sins.

Proverbs 10:12

Jesus in My Pocket

Just for You

Fold Here

FROM: ____________________

TO: ____________________

____

When I forgive from my heart...

I forgive the neighbor who does not act neighborly towards me. I do not become angry or vengeful, allowing someone else's actions to control my own.

God's Word says...

If you really fulfill the royal law according to the Scripture, "You shall love your neighbor as yourself," you do well.

James 2:8

Jesus in My Pocket

Just for You

Fold Here

FROM: ______________

TO: ______________

____

When I forgive from my heart...

I forgive those who do not show compassion to others. I ask the Lord to touch their hearts, open their eyes, and infuse their spirits with forgiveness.

God's Word says...

Thus says the LORD of hosts:
"Execute true justice,
Show mercy and compassion
Everyone to his brother."

Zechariah 7:9

Just for You

Jesus in My Pocket

Fold Here

FROM: ____________

TO: ____________

____

When I forgive from my heart...

My love for others grows. Because a forgiving heart allows the love of God to fill my soul, that same love will spill out to touch those around me.

God's Word says...

And above all things have fervent love for one another, for "love will cover a multitude of sins."

1 Peter 4:8

Just for You

Jesus in My Pocket

Fold Here

FROM: ____________________

TO: ____________________

____

When I forgive from my heart...

I forgive my family and friends when they aren't in my corner. When they knock my every effort and criticize me, I turn to the Lord for approval and forgive those on earth.

God's Word says...

For not he who commends himself is approved, but whom the Lord commends.

2 Corinthians 10:18

Just for You

Jesus in My Pocket

Fold Here

FROM: ____________________

TO: ____________________

____

When I forgive from my heart...

I forgive my children when they do not honor me. I remind them of God's law, remember that a parent is often the target of misdirected anger, and set a good example by honoring my own parents.

God's Word says...

And you, fathers, do not provoke your children to wrath, but bring them up in the training and admonition of the Lord.

Ephesians 6:4

Jesus in My Pocket

Just for You

Fold Here

FROM: ____________________

TO: ____________________

____

When I forgive from my heart...

I let go of the hurt and disappointment I feel when my children make unwise choices. I ask the Lord to help me guide them in their choices, to have them honor me as their parent, and to show them mercy when they stray from the right path.

God's Word says...

Train up a child in the way he should go,
And when he is old he will not depart
from it.

Proverbs 22:6

Jesus in My Pocket

Just for You

Fold Here

FROM: ____________

TO: ____________

____

When I forgive from my heart...

I forgive those who steal from me—whether they have stolen from my heart, my mind, or my possessions. I leave retaliation in the Lord's hands and pray that what is rightfully mine will be restored to me.

God's Word says...

Repay no one evil for evil. Have regard for good things in the sight of all men. . . . Do not be overcome by evil, but overcome evil with good.

Romans 12:17, 21

Just for You

Jesus in My Pocket

Fold Here

FROM: ____________

TO: ____________

____

When I forgive from my heart...

I forgive those who slander me. As a child of God, I know I was created in His perfect image, which lies and half-truths cannot destroy.

God's Word says...

For the Lord GOD will help Me;

Therefore I will not be disgraced;

Therefore I have set My face like a flint,

And I know I will not be ashamed.

Isaiah 50:7

Jesus in My Pocket

Just for You

Fold Here

FROM: ____________________

TO: ____________________

____

When I forgive from my heart...

I let go of the anger I feel towards those who have hurt me. I turn the other cheek and replace my hateful thoughts with love from a forgiving heart.

God's Word says...

If it is possible, as much as depends on you, live peaceably with all men. Beloved, do not avenge yourselves, but rather give place to wrath; for it is written, "Vengeance is Mine, I will repay," says the Lord.

Romans 12:18-19

Jesus in My Pocket

Just for You

Fold Here

FROM: ____________________

TO: ____________________

____

When I forgive from my heart...

I forgive those who don't forgive me. I know it's easier to be kind to those who treat me kindly, but I will make an effort to be loving to those who appear to be my enemies.

God's Word says...

But I say to you, love your enemies, bless those who curse you, do good to those who hate you, and pray for those who spitefully use you and persecute you.

Matthew 5:44

Jesus in My Pocket

Just for You

Fold Here

FROM: ____________________

TO: ____________________

____

When I forgive from my heart...

I forgive those who turn away from me when I'm in trouble. Their fear or insecurity might make them unable to comfort me, but whatever the reason, I remind myself it is Jesus' help I should be seeking.

God's Word says...

The LORD also will be a refuge for the
oppressed,
A refuge in times of trouble.
And those who know Your name will put
their trust in You;
For You, LORD, have not forsaken those
who seek You.

Psalm 9:9-10

Just for You

Jesus in My Pocket

Fold Here

FROM: ____________________

TO: ____________________

____

When I forgive from my heart...

I am filled with peace. I know I am practicing Jesus' law when I forgive, and my soul rests in peacefulness and contentment.

God's Word says...

You will keep him in perfect peace,
Whose mind is stayed on You,
Because he trusts in You.

Isaiah 26:3

Just for You

Jesus in My Pocket

Fold Here

FROM: ____________

TO: ____________

____

When I forgive from my heart...

I forgive those who laugh behind my back. From the bottom of my heart, I send them blessings and remember that they are only acting out of their own insecurities.

God's Word says...

The discretion of a man makes him slow
to anger,
And his glory is to overlook a
transgression.

Proverbs 19:11

Just for You

Jesus in My Pocket

Fold Here

FROM: ____________________

TO: ____________________

____

When I forgive from my heart...

I forgive those who are jealous of my talents. I know they have not yet discovered or appreciated the special talents God has given them, and I forgive them for envying mine.

God's Word says...

Let not the wise man glory in his wisdom,
Let not the mighty man glory in his might,
Nor let the rich man glory in his riches;
But let him who glories glory in this,
That he understands and knows Me,
That I am the LORD, exercising
lovingkindness, judgment, and
righteousness in the earth.

Jeremiah 9:23-24

Just for You

Jesus in My Pocket

Fold Here

FROM: ____________________

TO: ____________________

____

When I forgive from my heart...

I know my prayers are heard. I can breathe more easily and carry a song in my heart because heartfelt prayer cleanses and purifies me.

God's Word says...

But you, when you pray, go into your room, and when you have shut your door, pray to your Father who is in the secret place; and your Father who sees in secret will reward you openly.

Matthew 6:6

Jesus in My Pocket

Just for You

Fold Here

FROM: ____________________

TO: ____________________

____

When I forgive from my heart...

I forgive those who turn against me. Instead of getting angry, I pray for their peace and turn loving thoughts toward them.

God's Word says...

My beloved brethren, let every man be swift to hear, slow to speak, slow to wrath; for the wrath of man does not produce the righteousness of God.

James 1:19-20

Jesus in My Pocket

Just for You

Fold Here

FROM: ________________

TO: ________________

____

When I forgive from my heart...

I forgive my own lack of faith. I pray for guidance and direction from the Lord and ask Him to strengthen my belief in Him.

God's Word says...

Assuredly, I say to you, if you have faith as a mustard seed, you will say to this mountain, "Move from here to there," and it will move; and nothing will be impossible for you.

Matthew 17:20

Just for You

Jesus in My Pocket

Fold Here

FROM: ____________________

TO: ____________________

____

When I forgive from my heart...

I remain calm and centered during all life's storms. Knowing that the most perfect gift is forgiveness, I offer it with a loving heart.

God's Word says...

I have set the LORD always before me;

Because He is at my right hand I shall not be moved.

Psalm 16:8

To accept Jesus Christ as your personal Lord and Savior, pray out loud:

Heavenly Father,
I come to You in the name of Jesus. I believe in my heart that Jesus Christ is the Son of God, that He died on the Cross for my sins and was raised from the dead for my justification. I believe in my heart, and I now confess with my mouth that Jesus is Lord. Therefore, I am saved!